A Study Guide Based on the Best-selling Book

DR. LARRY CRABB

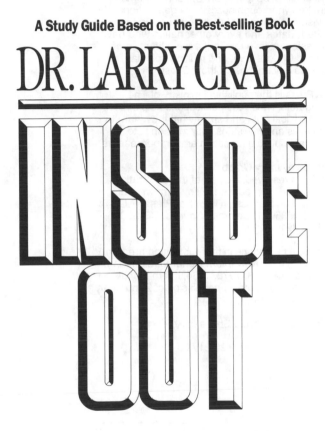

NAVPRESS ●®
A MINISTRY OF THE NAVIGATORS
P.O. BOX 35001, COLORADO SPRINGS, COLORADO 80935

The Navigators is an international Christian organization. Our mission is to reach, disciple, and equip people to know Christ and to make Him known through successive generations. We envision multitudes of diverse people in the United States and every other nation who have a passionate love for Christ, live a lifestyle of sharing Christ's love, and multiply spiritual laborers among those without Christ.

NavPress is the publishing ministry of The Navigators. NavPress publications help believers learn biblical truth and apply what they learn to their lives and ministries. Our mission is to stimulate spiritual formation among our readers.

Scripture quotations in this publication are from the *Holy Bible: New International Version* (NIV). Copyright © 1973, 1978, 1984, International Bible Society. Used by permission of Zondervan Bible Publishers.

Printed in the United States of America

15 16 17 18 19 20 21 / 00

Contents

Author

Dr. Larry Crabb is the founder and director of the Institute of Biblical Counseling, a ministry committed to training Christians to resolve life's problems biblically and to help others in the context of Christian community.

In addition to conducting IBC seminars across the country, Dr. Crabb serves as Chairman and Professor of the Graduate Department of Biblical Counseling at Colorado Christian University in Morrison, Colorado.

Dr. Crabb earned his Ph.D. in clinical psychology from the University of Illinois in 1970. He practiced psychology in Florida for ten years, and for seven years directed the Master's program in Biblical Counseling at Grace Theological Seminary in Winona Lake, Indiana.

Dr. Crabb's first book, *Basic Principles of Biblical Counseling*, was published in 1975, followed by *Effective Biblical Counseling*, *The Marriage Builder*, *Encouragment: The Key to Caring* (with Dan Allender), *Understanding People*, and *Men and Women: Enjoying The Difference*.

Dr. Crabb and his wife, Rachael, live in Frisco, Colorado. They have two sons, Keplen and Kenton.

How to Use This Guide

Ever since Jesus Christ ascended to the Father 2,000 years ago, Christians have been trying to understand what it means to be transformed into His image. What does it mean to grow, to change, to become the people of love and power He's called us to be?

Some say deep change comes through an exclusive focus on obedience to the Bible's commands. Others say it's the result of a mysterious inner working of the Holy Spirit. Still others say it comes through facing inner hurts and conflicts and overcoming them with the help of a professional.

Whatever the method, the modern consensus seems to be that when real change has taken place, it will no longer be necessary to wrestle with internal struggle and disorder. An inexpressible joy is available that, rather than *supporting* us through hard times, can actually *eliminate* pressure, worry, and pain from our experience. There is a solution to whatever ails us. Through trust in and obedience to Christ, relief will come.

Beneath much of our claim to orthodoxy, there is a moral cowardice that reflects poorly on our confidence in Christ. We trust Him to forgive our sins and to keep us more or less in line as a community of decent people, but is He enough to deal with things as they really are? Do we know

how to face the confusing reality of a world where good
parents sometimes have rebellious children and bad parents produce committed missionaries? Can we plunge into
the disturbing facts of life and emerge, as the writer of the
seventy-third Psalm did, with a renewed confidence in God
and a deeper thirst for Him? Can we enter those hidden
inner regions of our soul where emptiness is more the
reality than a consuming awareness of His presence and
where an honest look reveals that self-serving motives
stain even our noblest deeds? Is Christ enough to deal with
that kind of internal mess? Or is it better to never look at
all that and just get on with the Christian life?[1]

The book *Inside Out* has become a best seller because
many Christians are tired of pretending that things are better
than they are. They want to know Christ in a way that makes a
difference—not a difference in their world, but a difference in
themselves. They want to know how to face life honestly without crumbling, how to change without performing, how to love
others even when the risks are great. They're tired of burning
out on spiritual fads. They want truth. They want hope. They
want change—from the inside out.

Real change is possible. But it's different than you might
expect. And it takes a willingness to be ruthlessly honest with
yourself about the realities inside your soul and outside in your
world. The purpose of this guide is to help you begin to take
that honest look and move toward the kind of relationship with
Christ and others that will bring you the richest kind of life
possible.

Each lesson in this study is divided into five sections:

1. *An excerpt* from *Inside Out* that highlights the major
points from the corresponding chapter in the book. The book
contains much more helpful information than it was possible to
include in this guide, and reading the book as you're doing the
study will be important to your full understanding of the material. In many cases, you will need to read the book carefully in
order to answer the questions in the guide.

2. *Looking Inside.* The questions in this section will help
you reflect back on the excerpt you've just read and run it
through your personal "grid" of beliefs and emotions. Answer-

ing the questions will help you establish some kind of relationship with the material—congenial, adversarial, or neutral.

3. *Identifying the Problem.* This part of the lesson will take
you deeper into the message of the chapter, helping you draw
out main points and establish a clear understanding of the keys
to changing from the inside out. It's in answering the questions
in this section that you'll have to pay the closest attention to the
corresponding chapter in the book.

4. *Exploring Relationships.* The ultimate purpose of inside-
out change is love—being freed from the many things that trap
us behind styles of relating that keep genuine love from flow-
ing through us to others. Honestly answering the questions in
this section is crucial to your understanding of how all you're
learning in each lesson applies to your personal relationships.
Don't hurry through this part. Take a careful and thorough
inside look, and let God teach you more about living—by really
loving—in a disappointing world.

5. *Moving Toward Change.* This wrap-up section is
intended to help you identify any beliefs or feelings that may
be blocking your path to changing from the inside out. It will
also help you plan for ways to put what you've learned into
practice in your daily life. You may find your greatest encouragement in this section, so work through it carefully.

This guide can be used for individual study to great
benefit. You may gain even more from it, however, if you participate in a small group that works through it together. We can
all learn much from the experiences of others, and there's a lot
of support to be gained in group fellowship. Experience also
shows that in putting lessons learned into practice, we do much
better if we feel accountable to others—if we know someone
will ask us periodically how we're doing at putting our good
intentions into action.

You may find that your answers to some of the questions
are simply too personal to share with a group. Be honest with
your group about your feelings. The most important thing is to
begin being honest with yourself. Real change starts deep
inside, and it may take you some time before you'll feel ready
to share the deepest parts of yourself with others.

Thousands of Christians have already been deeply chal-
lenged and motivated by the message of *Inside Out.* This com-

panion study guide could be the tool you need to begin changing where the rubber meets the road. Real change *is* possible— if you're willing to start from the inside out.

NOTE: 1. Dr. Larry Crabb, *Inside Out* (Colorado Springs, Colo.: NavPress, 1988), page 15.

PART I

"Don't look inside me— I'm not sure I like what's there."
LOOKING BENEATH THE SURFACE OF LIFE

LESSON ONE

Real Change Requires an Inside Look

Just a quick glance beneath the surface of our life makes it clear that more is going on than loving God and loving others. It requires only a moment of honest self-reflection to realize that, no matter how much we may have already changed, we still have a long way to go. Most of us know things about ourself that no one else would guess: thoughts, fantasies, things we do in private, secrets that make us feel ashamed. We know things are not as they should be. Something is wrong. . . .

When we succeed at arranging our life so that "all is well," we keep ourself from facing all that's going on inside. And when we ignore what's happening on the inside, we lose all power to change what we do on the outside in any meaningful way. We *rearrange* rather than *change*, and in so doing, we never become the transformed person God calls us to be. We never experience freedom from destructive patterns of living. . . .

In His rebuke to the Pharisees, our Lord declared a principle that must guide all our efforts to change into the person God wants us to be. He made it clear that there is no place for pretense. We must come to grips with what's going on behind the whitewashed appearance of our life. It seems to be His teaching that we can't make it if we don't face all that we are. To look honestly at those parts of our experience we naturally deny is painful business, so painful that the analogy of death is not too strong. But to change according to Christ's instructions requires us to face all we prefer to deny. *Real change requires an inside look.*[1]

LOOKING INSIDE

1. a. Do you agree that things are not as they should be in

your personal life?

b. What is going on in your life—thoughts, desires, behaviors, attitudes—that surprises or frustrates you?

2. a. What are some of your destructive patterns of living—that others may or may not be aware of?

b. What are some ways you've *rearranged* your behavior rather than *changed* on the inside?

3. What scares or disturbs you most about taking an inside look?

IDENTIFYING THE PROBLEM

4. a. Using the scale below, what rating would you give yourself on how well you understand what's going on inside
you—your motives, emotions, desires, and disappointments?

1   2   3   4   5   6   7   8   9   10

Not at all   Perfectly well

b. What rating would you give yourself on how well you
understood your "inside self" five years ago?

1   2   3   4   5   6   7   8   9   10

Not at all   Perfectly well

5. a. In what group of people would you place yourself at this
point in your Christian life?

__ Those who are trying hard to do what the Bible commands but feel frustrated.
__ Those who are doing quite well and feel content and
happy most of the time.
__ Those who are hardened and disillusioned.
__ Those who are in positions of Christian leadership and
feel pressure to perform.

b. What do you feel you most need to experience right
now? Why?

__ Hope
__ More
__ Life
__ Love

6. a. Read Matthew 23:25-26. What was Jesus criticizing in the
Pharisees' lives?

b. Why do you think His rebuke was so harsh?

c. Why is change from the inside out so important?

7. "Too often, a commitment to obedience reflects not a passionate desire to pursue God, but a stubbornly fearful
   determination to not feel deep frustration and personal
   pain. When the energy behind our obedience is supplied by
   the desire to deny pain, the warm, fleshy parts of the human
   soul are not engaged in following God."[2]

   a. In what ways does your obedience to God result from
      spiritual passion or from fear? How do you know?

   b. What are some of the characteristics of a Christian who is
      not committed to self-protection?

EXPLORING RELATIONSHIPS

8. "We live for the purpose of self-protection, clinging to whatever brings us happiness and security. The effect is a discouraging distance between ourself and the people we long to be close to. The quality of our life diminishes."[3]

   a. Can you identify a commitment to self-protection in your life? If so, describe it.

   b. How would you rate your quality of life? On what basis?

9. a. Read John 15:12-13, Galatians 5:13-14, and 1 Peter 1:22. What is the measure of our obedience to God?

   b. As you think about your relationships, in what ways can you honestly say they are characterized by a pure, Christlike love on your part?

   c. What *does* characterize your way of relating to people?

10. a. Think about the person to whom you are closest. Describe the last time you responded to that person more out of self-protection than love.

b. What motivated your self-protective attitude or behavior?

MOVING TOWARD CHANGE

11. a. Would you categorize yourself more as a *shallow coper* or a *troubled reflecter*?

b. Why are troubled reflecters more likely to experience real change?

12. a. What brings you the greatest joy—comfortable circumstances, rich relationships, or deep communion with God?

b. How does your approach to life and relationships reflect your true values?

13. a. In what ways are you pretending that things are better than they are?

b. How does pretense prevent change from the inside out?

14. a. What do the following verses suggest about a starting place for change?

James 1:5

James 4:10

b. What are two things you can do to begin your journey?

NOTES: 1. Dr. Larry Crabb, *Inside Out* (Colorado Springs, Colo.: NavPress, 1988), pages 29, 31, 33.
   2. Page 36.
   3. Page 30.

An Inside Look
Can Be Frustrating

For centuries Christians have grappled with how we are to work out our own salvation (which seems to involve real effort) while somehow depending on God to work inside us, enabling us by His strength to desire and carry out His will. If we are to be more than humanistic, relying on our own resources to become all we can be, then *dependence on God* as we seek to obey Him must go beyond inspiring rhetoric. It must become vital reality.

But just how do we depend completely on God? The answer is elusive. . . . And because it's elusive, most modern approaches to understanding ourself and changing come back to the central ingredient of effort. Whether our problem is doing something we wish we weren't doing, or wanting to completely surrender ourself to God, or struggling to believe we really are loved by God, the bottom line is still the same: TRY HARDER![1]

LOOKING INSIDE

1. a. What does it mean for you to depend on God?

b. Is dependence on God a vital reality in your life?

c. How is dependence developed in a Christian's life?

2. a. What have you learned about cooperating with God in order to change an attitude or behavior? Give a specific example.

b. How do human effort and depending on God's power fit together?

3. a. What are the biggest problem areas that you're aware of in your life?

b. How have you approached changing them so far?

IDENTIFYING THE PROBLEM

4. What are some of the "above-the-waterline" issues—actions, thoughts, and feelings—that you feel able to control or change through effort? (In other words, what are some areas in which you feel pretty "together"?)

5. a. What are some "below-the-waterline" issues—motives, urges, memories, and attitudes—that no amount of effort seems to control consistently? The list below may help you identify some of them.

Resentment	Homosexual urges	Urges to do violence
Boredom	Low motivation	Fatigue
Fear	Self-pity	Inability to feel close
Lack of love	Low self-esteem	to others

b. How do you feel about these more covert problems and your ability to change them?

6. a. On what do you *most* base your hope for changing "below-the-waterline" problems?

__ Diligent performance of Christian duties
__ A definitive work of the Holy Spirit
__ Some form of counseling

__ Other _____

b. Which of these options requires an inside look?

c. Do you agree that each option is inadequate? Why or why not?

EXPLORING RELATIONSHIPS

7. "Our Lord made it clear that doing right in His eyes required far more than the performance of certain activities. The entire law, He said, could be summarized in two commands: Love God and love others. We cannot honor these exhortations in even the smallest measure without profound internal change. Moral effort alone can never produce genuine love."[2]

a. Give an example from your life of a time when trying harder to be loving toward someone failed to produce genuinely loving attitudes and motives.

b. What do you think your chances are of doing better next time?

8. "When we're convinced that every problem in living, both between people and within them, reflects a style of relating that violates God's standards of love, and when we see that learning to love is an inside job requiring far more than moral effort, we will be eager to take an inside look."[3]

Think about some of the problems below and how they might be rooted in styles of relating that violate love.

Anorexia	Drug abuse	Marital discord
Anxiety	Homosexuality	Outbursts of temper
Depression	Loneliness	Overeating

What problem in your own life might be rooted in an unloving style of relating?

9. a. What do the following verses say about the role of other people in helping us face the truth about ourselves?

Proverbs 20:5

James 5:16

b. What part can others play in our process of changing from the inside out?

MOVING TOWARD CHANGE

10. What do you see as the essential differences between *doing* good and *being* good?

11. a. Whose patterns of behavior do you most respect?

b. Whose character qualities do you most admire?

c. Which person(s) most inspires you to change? Why?

12. In what ways are you substituting "cosmetic surgery" for the profound internal change God wants for your life?

13. a. What is a character quality that seems sorely missing from your life?

b. How can you begin to develop it?

NOTES: 1. Dr. Larry Crabb, *Inside Out* (Colorado Springs, Colo.: NavPress, 1988), pages 42-43.
2. Page 43.
3. Page 43.

Knowing What to Look For

The human race got off on a seriously wrong foot when Eve yielded to Satan's lie that more satisfaction was available if she took matters into her own hands. When Adam joined her in looking for life outside of God's revealed will, he infected all his descendants with the disease of self-management. Now no one seeks after God in an effort to find life. The most natural thing for us to do is to develop strategies for finding life that reflect our commitment to depending on our own resources. Simple trust is out of fashion. Self-protection has become the norm.

The Scriptures consistently expose people as both thirsty and foolish. We long for the satisfaction we were built to enjoy, but we all move away from God to find it. An inside look, then, can be expected to uncover two elements imbedded deeply in our heart: (1) thirst or *deep longings* for what we do not have; and (2) stubborn independence reflected in *wrong strategies* for finding the life we desire. . . .

An inside look must anticipate uncovering both deep, unsatisfied longings that bear testimony to our *dignity*, as well as foolish and ineffective strategies for keeping ourself out of pain that reflect our *depravity*. Each of us is a glorious ruin. And the further we look into our heart, the more clearly we can see the wonder of our ability to enjoy relationship alongside the tragedy of our determination to arrange for our own protection from hurt.[1]

LOOKING INSIDE

1. In what areas of your life are you most tempted to depend on something or someone other than Christ for deep satis-

faction and a reason for living?

Think about relationships with others as you answer questions 2 and 3.

2. a. What are the most commonly recurring desires in your life?

   b. How have you attempted to satisfy them?

3. a. What are the most commonly recurring disappointments in your life?

   b. How have you attempted to protect yourself from being hurt in the same way again?

IDENTIFYING THE PROBLEM

4. a. Read Proverbs 4:23 and Jeremiah 17:9. What do these verses suggest about the difficulty of identifying our wrong strategies for finding life?

   b. What do the following verses tell us we can depend on for the information we need about ourselves that enables us to begin changing from the inside out?

   Psalm 139:23-24

   Hebrews 4:12

5. a. Are you "thirsty"? Why?

   b. Is everyone thirsty this side of Heaven?

   c. Is it wrong to be thirsty? Why or why not?

6. What are you thirsty for? (What do you most long for that you do not have?) What is "life" for you?

7. a. Read Jeremiah 2:13. In what ways have you "dug your own cisterns"?

   b. Why is it sinful to dig our own wells?

8. a. What measure of fulfillment have you experienced through your strategies to find life?

   b. How does digging our own wells reveal our foolishness?

EXPLORING RELATIONSHIPS

9. What relationships have caused you the most pain, and why?

10. What is your normal response when you're deeply disappointed in some relationship?

11. a. How important are meaningful relationships to you?

    b. What is at the root of your disappointment in other people's responses to you?

12. Identify some ways you protect yourself from potential disappointment and pain in your relationships.

MOVING TOWARD CHANGE

13. a. Is it difficult for you to trust God with your relationships? Why or why not?

    b. In what ways do you trust Him?

    c. In what ways do you not?

14. a. What example can you give of an action you took in the past week that was motivated primarily by love?

   b. What example can you give of an action motivated primarily by self-protection?

15. Is it really wrong to protect ourselves from pain in relationships, or are there times when self-protection is okay? Why do you think so?

16. a. What example can you give of a time when the deceitfulness of your heart became apparent to you?

   b. How did you respond to that realization?

17. a. How willing are you to explore your deep longings and
    wrong strategies?

   b. At this point in your study, how do you feel about the
   process involved in changing from the inside out?

NOTE: 1. Dr. Larry Crabb, *Inside Out* (Colorado Springs, Colo.: NavPress, 1988), pages
        54-55.

PART II

"I don't want to admit it— but I know something's wrong."
WE'RE THIRSTY PEOPLE

LESSON FOUR

"If Anyone Is Thirsty . . ."

Two categories of Christians emerge: those who have high standards of commitment and those who are content to live ordinary, respectable lives. The first group includes people who are frustrated with their inability to measure up to their lofty ideals and a few who are satisfied with their performance. The second group consists mostly of folks who live reasonably happy lives as long as money, health, and relationships are doing well. If things fall apart, they scramble to restore a measure of order to their lives. If that proves impossible, then a search for alternative sources of comfort begins. When available comfort is exceeded by inescapable suffering, then bitterness, depression, and a commitment to escape develop. . . .

. . . Notice carefully that a zeal for measuring up to standards did not produce the kind of life our Lord commended. And the ordinary people, folks who were more relaxed than committed, made the Lord gag. Outside cleanliness, whether the product of zeal or of complacency, does not impress our Lord. With relentless penetration, He intends to deal with the filth we try to keep hidden beneath the surface. To live life as God intends requires that we uncover the dirt and learn what we must do to participate in the cleaning process. We must take an inside look.[1]

LOOKING INSIDE

1. What category of Christian do you most identify with—the group that has a high level of commitment to measure up to God's standards, or the group that is content to live ordinary, respectable lives?

2. a. If you are in the first group, do you often feel frustrated in your efforts to live up to God's ideals?

   b. How do you feel about the news that trying harder to do what's right doesn't produce the kind of life that most pleases God?

3. If you are in the second group, how do you feel about the news that God intends to penetrate below the surface of your complacency and expose the issues that need to be dealt with?

IDENTIFYING THE PROBLEM

4. Read John 6:35-36. Is the fact that we're hungry and thirsty a problem? What *is* the problem?

5. Why does becoming passionately aware of our longings put us in touch with pain?

6. a. When we deny our longings, what suffers in our relationships with God and with other people?

b. Give examples from your own life.

7. a. On the scale below, indicate how aware you feel of your deep longings.

1   2   3   4   5   6   7   8   9   10
Very unaware   Very aware

b. How aware are you of your disappointments?

1   2   3   4   5   6   7   8   9   10
Very unaware   Very aware

c. What is the result in your life of this combination? In other words, how do you feel about and deal with the disappointment of your longings?

8. "When relieving pain is not our final purpose in life, then it's reasonable to make ourself as comfortable as a responsible and moral approach to life permits. *But when relief of the inevitable pain of living in a fallen world becomes our priority, at that moment we leave the path toward pursuing God.*"[2]

a. Do you agree with this statement? Why or why not?

b. When does relieving our pain cease to be "reasonable" and become sinful?

c. How committed are you to relieving the ache in your soul as you live this side of Heaven? How do you know you are committed?

EXPLORING RELATIONSHIPS

9. a. What are the two things human beings most crave?

b. Do we ever get enough of these two things? Why or why not?

10. Read Genesis 2:18-25. What elements in this first recorded relationship reflect the ideal God had in mind?

11. a. Do any of your relationships reflect all of these ideals?

b. Why is it natural for you to be hurt by less-than-perfect relationships?

12. a. Are you aware of an emptiness at the core of your being?

   b. How does that emptiness influence the way you approach people and God?

13. a. What example can you give of a time within the past week when you became aware of how badly someone failed you?

   b. How did you respond?

MOVING TOWARD CHANGE

14. a. What is your definition of maturity?

   b. How far along the road toward maturity do you feel you are?

c. How do you measure your progress?

15. "The simple fact we must face is this: *Something is wrong
    with everything.* No matter how closely we walk with the
    Lord, we cannot escape the impact of a disappointing and
    sometimes evil world. A core sadness that will not go away
    is evidence not of spiritual immaturity, but of honest living
    in a sad world."[3]

    a. Do you agree that "something is wrong with everything"?
       Why or why not?

    b. Are you aware of a core sadness within you that never
       completely goes away? Why can that sadness be a positive
       thing?

16. Read John 7:37-38 and 16:20-22. What encouragement do
    these verses give as we live this side of Heaven?

17. a. Do you feel pressure to feel good all the time because
       you're a Christian?

b. How can what you've learned so far in this study free you
to relax with the fact that you feel disappointed by a disappointing world?

NOTES: 1. Dr. Larry Crabb, *Inside Out* (Colorado Springs, Colo.: NavPress, 1988), page 62.
       2. Pages 73-74.
       3. Page 74.

Springs of Living Water? Then Why So Much Pain?

I f we are to become a community of deeply changed people, we must not only admit to our thirst, we must carefully explore what Christ promised to do about that thirst. Did He promise to bring us comfort through enjoyable relationships, rewarding careers, and pleasurable activities—provided, of course, that we honor some level of commitment to Him? Or is the abundant life of bubbling springs a very different matter? Is it possible to have absolutely no rich communication with your husband, yet still taste those cool waters? Can a parent whose young adult son is far from the Lord know something real about peace and rest?

Our Lord has promised to flood our innermost being with springs of living water. If His words do not guarantee our personal comfort in exchange for spiritual commitment—and I don't think they do—then what is He saying? If He's promised springs of living water to all who come, then why do many sincere Christians live lives filled with pain?[1]

LOOKING INSIDE

1. What have you understood the "abundant life" to consist of?

2. a. What, if anything, has led you to believe that your commitment to obeying God would result in material and
relational blessings from God?

   b. In what ways have you been disappointed in the "pay-
off" of the Christian life?

3. a. Do you believe it's possible to have real joy and peace
amidst painful circumstances and disappointing
relationships?

   b. To what extent has this been your experience?

IDENTIFYING THE PROBLEM

4. a. What do the following verses imply about the rewards for
following Christ?

   Matthew 6:25-33

   Romans 8:28-29

   Philippians 4:19

b. What do you think God is really promising in these verses?

5. What are the three levels of longings? What are the consequences when these longings go unmet?

LEVELS OF LONGINGS	CONSEQUENCES OF DISAPPOINTMENT

6. a. What level of longings are you most aware of on a daily basis?

b. What longings do you expend the most energy in trying to fill?

7. a. What were some of your casual longings this past week?

b. What were some of your critical longings?

c. When was the last time you were deeply aware of your crucial longings?

8. a. When in the past week did you experience manageable discomfort because a casual longing went unsatisfied?

b. When did you experience an immobilizing lostness because a critical longing went unmet?

c. How did you handle your disappointment?

9. a. At this time in your life, how satisfied do you feel in the areas of your casual longings, your critical longings, and your crucial longings?

1	2	3	4	5	6	7	8	9	10

Very unsatisfied   Very satisfied

b. How satisfied did you feel at these three levels three years ago?

1	2	3	4	5	6	7	8	9	10

Very unsatisfied   Very satisfied

EXPLORING RELATIONSHIPS

10. "Fullness in the outer two circles is often mistaken for the inexpressible joy of knowing the Lord. Enjoying the sought-after *blessings* of God is sometimes confused with enjoying His *Person*."[2]

  a. Think of a time in the past year when you felt deeply satisfied. What were your circumstances? How were your relationships going? What was going on in your relationship with God?

  b. Describe the last time you deeply enjoyed the *Person* of God, apart from His blessings. How satisfied did you feel in His presence?

11. What are some ways you go about getting your critical longings met on a daily basis?

12. a. What is the inevitable result of banking our happiness on the fulfillment of our casual and critical longings?

 b. Why is experiencing dissatisfaction of our critical longings so important in driving us to God?

 c. When did you last depend on God more fully because of disappointment in an important human relationship?

13. a. What pretenses have sprung up in your thoughts, attitudes, or behavior because of an unwillingness to face head-on some hurt in your life?

 b. What is the potential positive result of facing our disappointment in relationships?

MOVING TOWARD CHANGE

14. How honest do you feel you've been so far in your life in facing your disappointments?

1   2   3   4   5   6   7   8   9   10
Very dishonest   Completely honest

15. a. To what extent has facing the dissatisfaction of your casual and critical longings moved you to a deeper sense of fulfillment of your crucial longings?

    b. In general, why has facing disappointment moved you closer to God, or away from God?

16. a. On what or whom besides God do you depend for the satisfaction of your crucial longings?

    b. How has this misplaced dependence led to frustration, bitterness, fear, self-reproach, or depression?

17. a. What longings has God promised to satisfy?

    b. What longings has He not promised to satisfy in the ways we might hope?

18. What is the potential result of being free of our preoccupation with the frustration of our longings?

19. What have you learned so far in your study about the process of change from the inside out? (Can you identify three essential elements?)

NOTES: 1. Dr. Larry Crabb, *Inside Out* (Colorado Springs, Colo.: NavPress, 1988), page 80.
    2. Page 84.

Becoming Aware of Our Thirst

There is incredible resistance, more in Christian circles, I think, than in secular, to owning internal pain. Even a glance in the direction of discouragement and fear violates our idea of what a victorious Christian should be doing. . . .

Many Christians manage to keep life moving along rather smoothly without ever looking deeply at the pain in their souls. And the ones who do take a look sometimes crumble under the weight of what they discover. Why, then, take an inside look? If all it achieves is a greater awareness of unbelievable sorrow, why bother? Isn't it cruel to remind a desert traveler how parched his throat feels? Yes. If the only effect of becoming aware of our thirst is to heighten our misery, then it's stupid and wrong to look inside. On the other hand, if an awareness of our thirst is the beginning of closer fellowship with God (at whose right hand are abundant pleasures), then it makes sense. It is worth whatever temporary pain is stirred up, no matter how untemporary or severe the pain might seem.

The choice before us is rather stark: either live to be comfortable (both internally and externally, but especially internally), or live to know God. We can't have it both ways. One choice excludes the other.[1]

LOOKING INSIDE

1. a. To what degree is there a resistance by Christians to owning internal pain?

b. Have you observed this resistance in yourself? If so, why is it there?

2. Do you believe an inside look at personal pain and problems is the beginning of closer fellowship with God and more abundant living—or a detour toward these goals? Why?

3. Do you believe that pursuing personal comfort and pursuing a meaningful relationship with God are diametrically opposed? Why or why not?

IDENTIFYING THE PROBLEM

4. a. Why does attempting to satisfy our crucial longings with anything but Christ often lead to compulsive behavior?

b. How can facing the disappointment of our longings keep us from being enslaved by habitual sin?

5. a. Is there anything in your life—thoughts, behaviors, people—to which you feel addicted or enslaved?

   b. What connection, if any, do you see between your predicament and your failure to deal with the disappointment of your deepest longings for relationship?

6. a. What do you consider to be the greatest sins of your life, past and present?

   b. Are these sins "above the waterline" or below it?

7. a. How would you define the sin of self-protection?

   b. Why is it a sin?

   c. How can facing our thirst help us identify the subtle sin of self-protection in the ways we relate to people?

8. a. What do the following verses reveal about the writers'
dependence on God?

Job 19:25-27

Psalm 42:1-2

Psalm 63:1

b. To what extent do you share these writers' passion for
God?

9. "God longs for us to give our heart to Him. He loves us. To
the degree that we embrace our thirst and realize who He
is, we long for Him. There is nothing dull about the
romance between our heavenly Bridegroom and His hurting
but fickle bride. The more honestly we face whatever hurt
may be locked inside, the more passionately we can be
drawn to the beauty of a Lover who responds consistently
with all the tender strength our heart desires."[2]

How can you begin to develop a more meaningful,
exciting love relationship with Christ?

EXPLORING RELATIONSHIPS

10. a. Think of a person who entices you to know Christ better.
What is it about that person that draws you to the Lord?

    b. In what way does that person seem to acknowledge and
    embrace the pain in their own soul?

11. Why does protecting ourself from the pain of our disappointed longings blunt our capacity to love?

12. a. Describe a time this past week when protecting yourself
kept you from moving toward someone else in genuine
love.

    b. What were you protecting yourself from?

    c. What commitment was at the root of your self-protection?

13. What styles of relating—friendliness, humor, shyness, etc.—do you use to protect yourself from hurt?

14. How often do you feel you genuinely and freely love other human beings?

1	2	3	4	5	6	7	8	9	10
Almost never									Almost always

15. In your life, how would giving up self-protection alter your style of relating? Give a specific example.

MOVING TOWARD CHANGE

16. a. Why will an honest look at life produce confusion?

    b. What are some ways people try to avoid feeling confused?

17. a. Let your mind explore some of the hard issues and experiences in your life. How do you feel about them?

b. How have you coped with your feelings thus far?

18. a. What is the only thing that can satisfy us when we feel overwhelmingly confused?

    b. Why?

19. a. What is the purpose of admitting how disappointed we are in all our relationships?

    b. What is the only antidote for disappointment and the demandingness it creates?

20. a. How can studying our style of relating to others produce conviction?

    b. What, if anything, do you feel convicted about in your approach to relationships?

21. The route to facing our thirst involves three crucial actions, results in three responses or states of mind, and opens us to discover three antidotes. See if you can retrace this route on the chart below.

ACTION	RESPONSE	ANTIDOTE

NOTES: 1. Dr. Larry Crabb, *Inside Out* (Colorado Springs, Colo.: NavPress, 1988), pages 90-91.
2. Page 102.

PART III

"Even when I get what I want— it's not what I want."
DIGGING BROKEN WELLS

Looking in All the Wrong Places

S o much more is involved in changing from the inside out than pulling rotten fruit off the tree. Our struggle against sin requires a far tougher battle than the struggle to do right and not do wrong. . . .

. . . [God] requires us to look carefully at our approach to relationships to see where self-interest corrupts love. The whole purpose of the law is to point the way toward quality relationships with God and others. In order to understand what the invitation to come entails, we must go beyond a legitimate concern with visible sin and explore the ways in which thirsty people who desperately want relationship foolishly violate the command to love. . . .

Change from the inside out requires that we look beneath the surface of life to see not only the deep longings of our thirsty soul but also the self-protective commitments of our deceitful heart.[1]

LOOKING INSIDE

1. Do you agree that the whole purpose of the law is to guide us into quality relationships? Why or why not?

2. Do you feel that self-protection is as serious a problem as this study suggests? Why or why not?

3. Which is more difficult for you to face: the fact that you have deep longings, or self-protective commitments? Why?

IDENTIFYING THE PROBLEM

4. a. Read Matthew 23:23. What was Jesus rebuking the Pharisees about?

  b. What does His rebuke indicate about the focus He wants Christians to have?

5. a. How do you know when you have violated the law of love?

  b. Give an example of a time when you violated love during the past week. (Go beyond naming an obviously unkind action; identify the self-protective motive behind an action that was unloving whether or not it appeared so on the surface.)

6. In what way does a priority effort to play it safe interfere with the purpose of living?

7. "We were designed by a God who wants us to trust His love enough to freely love others, not to protect our longings from further injury. And yet we love so poorly. Why? The answer is as simple as it is profound. We refuse to come to God in our thirst by abandoning our commitment to self-protection. Instead, we read our Bible and burn our porno magazines. We walk past the well of God to grab a shovel and begin digging for water in our relationships.

"How foolish! But worse, how *subtly* we dig our broken wells."[2]

a. Describe some ways a commitment to self-protection is demonstrated in your life on a daily basis.

b. What are some examples—both obvious and subtle—of times you have dug broken wells rather than come to Christ with your thirst?

EXPLORING RELATIONSHIPS

8. Think of your style of relating. Do you have more than one? Describe the circumstances that draw out each particular style.

9. If you are doing this study in a group, ask the group members for feedback on your relational style. Also ask for feedback from others who know you well and observe you in a variety of situations. How do you feel about others' descriptions of your relational style—encouraged, discouraged, defensive, hurt?

10. What appears to be the *function* of your relational style(s)? (What does it protect you from?)

11. a. According to Ephesians 4:15-16, is it wrong to be an individual with a unique style and function?

    b. Why did God create each of us to function in different ways?

c. How do we know when we are relating according to
God's design, or sinning through our relational style?

12. a. What deep longings preoccupy you enough to hinder
your freedom in truly loving others?

b. What risks do you feel you're taking when you move
toward others in love?

13. How committed do you feel you are to self-protection?

1	2	3	4	5	6	7	8	9	10

Not at all committed   Extremely committed

MOVING TOWARD CHANGE

14. How does denying our thirst keep us from recognizing the
function of our relational style?

15. a. Which do we most need to deal with: our style of relating, or the purpose it serves? Why?

b. Why is recognizing the sin of self-protection such a crucial step in changing from the inside out?

16. a. What is the mark of maturity (John 13:35)?

   b. What is the essence of love (John 15:13)?

17. a. As you contemplate moving out into your world without self-protective strategies, how do you feel?

   b. Where do you truly believe life can be found: in avoiding pain, or in loving God and others? Why?

   c. What stops you from relinquishing your commitment to self-protection?

NOTES: 1. Dr. Larry Crabb, *Inside Out* (Colorado Springs, Colo.: NavPress, 1988), pages 114, 116.
       2. Page 120.

The Problem of Demandingness

S incere Christians who want to change are given two options: Find help as you honestly explore the *pain in your heart*, or assume responsibility for straightening out the *sin in your behavior*. Pain in the heart and sin in behavior: two categories we need to deal with. And yet neither one guides us into the deep parts of our soul that are ugly, deformed, and diseased. Neither one helps us penetrate into the *sin in our heart* that must be addressed if we are to change from the inside out. Sin involves far more than its outward expression (sin in behavior), and we struggle against worse problems than deeply imbedded psychological hang-ups (pain in the heart).

. . . The problem in our heart is far worse than many suspect. When we look inside, we'll bump into more than bad memories and painful feelings. An honest look will in every case eventually expose something terribly ugly—something I want to label demandingness.[1]

LOOKING INSIDE

1. a. Up to this point in your life, what have you spent the most time and energy dealing with: the pain in your heart, or the sin in your behavior?

b. What are some of the tacks you have taken to deal with these problems?

2. a. What are some of the ways you've been sinned against by others?

b. What would you say have been your greatest sins against others?

3. What do you believe trips you up the most in your attempts to grow as a Christian?

IDENTIFYING THE PROBLEM

4. What causes us to be demanding people? (What is the root of the problem?)

5. Think of a few times when you felt justified in demanding that God answer your prayers. What were you praying for?

6. a. What do the following verses reveal about Jesus' submission to the authority of the Father?

   Luke 22:42

   Philippians 2:5-8

   b. What was the primary characteristic of Jesus' attitude?

7. a. When in our lives does the temptation to be demanding become the strongest?

   b. Why do you think this is so?

8. Think of a time when you were particularly frustrated or in pain over circumstances in your life.

   a. How long did these painful circumstances last?

b. How did you initially respond to the problem?

c. How did you feel and respond as time wore on and God did not quickly answer your prayers for relief?

9. Read Job 13:3. Think of a time when you felt like arguing your case with God. What was going on in your life?

10. "Notice the central problem: It is neither the hurt in our soul (it's okay to hurt) nor our desire for relief and satisfaction (it's okay to thirst); it is the *demand.* When we demand relief of our thirst now, we're in danger of slipping from a biblical ethic into a morality of pragmatism: whatever eases our pain is justified. The result is often blatant moral compromise and a ruined life. Others who both hurt and demand may not turn their backs on God by living in obvious sin, but they continue to deal with Him from the premise that their demands have merit."[2]

a. What is your emotional response to this assertion?

b. What feelings do you have when you realize that God has not always cooperated with your plans?

c. How would you describe your present attitude toward God and your approach to relationship with Him?

EXPLORING RELATIONSHIPS

11. In what ways are you most tempted to put pressure on others to respect, understand, or serve you?

12. a. Describe the last time you were angry or disappointed in someone.

b. In what way did their action or failure threaten your well-being or thwart your goals?

c. How did you respond to them?

13. Is protecting ourself from someone who's let us down ever justified? Why or why not?

14. a. How do you know when you've crossed the line between *legitimately desiring* that circumstances or people change and *illegitimately demanding* that they do?

b. Why is demanding illegitimate?

15. Think of a relationship in your life that is not going well. What has been your strategy for dealing with it?

MOVING TOWARD CHANGE

16. Do you agree with the statement, "*To trust God means to demand nothing*"? Why or why not?

17. a. As you reflect on your life, how completely do you feel you trust God with every part of it?

     1   2   3   4   5   6   7   8   9   10
     Not at all   Completely

   b. How completely did you trust God with your life three years ago?

     1   2   3   4   5   6   7   8   9   10
     Not at all   Completely

   c. If your level of trust has increased or decreased, explain the reasons for the change.

18. a. Does trusting God mean we never feel anguish or long for relief?

   b. Describe a time in your life when you trusted God in the midst of troubling circumstances or deep pain. What were you trusting Him for?

19. According to Psalm 111:10 and Proverbs 1:7, what must come before the potential for deep change is possible?

20. In Job 42:1-6, what was Job repenting of?

21. a. What encouraging promise is given in Isaiah 33:6?

b. What is the condition for the fulfillment of this promise?

NOTES: 1. Dr. Larry Crabb, *Inside Out* (Colorado Springs, Colo.: NavPress, 1988), page 132.
2. Page 143.

Exposing Wrong Directions

A determination to maintain personal safety, no matter how attractively disguised, is always ugly. To demand anything, including what we believe is essential to our well-being, reflects arrogant pride, a sin that tops the list of what God detests. Yet sin in the heart so often goes unnoticed. Very few people seem concerned with the possibility that their approach to relationships may be seriously deficient. We simply do not see, nor do we care to, that the way we "come across" to others may grow out of a demanding commitment to self-preservation lodged stubbornly in our heart. . . .

We simply must get to the core of the matter. The kind of change that most delights our Lord will never occur as long as we fuss *only* with sin in behavior or pain in the heart. *Sin* in the heart must be uncovered, looked at, and dealt with. When we understand we're thirsty people who foolishly go in wrong directions to find water, then we can look at our style of relating with an openness to recognizing a demanding, self protective motive beneath our actions.[1]

LOOKING INSIDE

1. Do you agree that demanding even what seems essential to your well-being is a heinous sin? Why or why not?

2. a. How much of the time do you think a demanding, self-protective motive fuels your interactions with others?

1   2   3   4   5   6   7   8   9   10
Almost never   Almost always

  b. To what extent does this indicate that your approach to relationships is or is not seriously deficient?

IDENTIFYING THE PROBLEM

3. a. What are the dangers of carefully evaluating our relational style?

  b. What is the sole value of an inside look?

4. a. How much do you desire to know yourself and why you do the things you do?

1   2   3   4   5   6   7   8   9   10
Not much   A lot

  b. How do you know if your goal in life is comfort in this world, or conformity to Christ?

5. a. How would you define *sin in the heart*?

   b. Are you often convicted of this kind of sin?

   c. How often do you ask the Spirit of God to expose the ways in which you sinfully relate to others?

6. a. When you read your Bible, what is your goal?

   b. In what ways do you feel that your knowledge of Scripture deeply influences the way you live your life?

EXPLORING RELATIONSHIPS

7. What do the following verses suggest about our responsibility to other believers?

   Matthew 18:15

   Galatians 6:1-2

Hebrews 3:12-13

James 5:14-16

8. a. Which people in your life know you well enough to confront you about the specific ways, both obvious and subtle, in which you violate the command to love?

b. Who do you know well enough to confront on the same issues?

9. Think about the individuals and groups with whom you are involved. On the scale below, indicate how deep you feel your closest relationships are in terms of mutual encouragement to change from the inside out.

1   2   3   4   5   6   7   8   9   10

Superficial, no power   Deep, powerful

10. How open are you to receiving feedback from others about your disobedience to biblical standards (sin in your behavior), and about your relational style (sin in your heart)?

11. a. How regularly do you give others feedback about sin in their lives?

b. When you do confront someone, what is your motive?

MOVING TOWARD CHANGE

12. At this point in your life, what do you most depend on for insight about what needs to be changed in your life?

13. What does it mean to come to the Word of God with integrity?

14. a. Are you willing to deeply involve yourself with other believers for the purpose of helping each other become less self-protective?

    b. If not, why not?

    c. What concerns or frightens you most about interaction at this level?

15. If you are not already involved in relationships that touch you deeply and encourage you to change from the inside out, think of someone with whom you'd like to relate at this level. What steps could you take to begin moving into a deeper relationship with this person?

NOTE: 1. Dr. Larry Crabb, *Inside Out* (Colorado Springs, Colo.: NavPress, 1988), pages 154, 156.

PART IV

"How can I make it—
if I face all that's going on inside?"
CHANGING FROM THE INSIDE OUT

Defining the Problem

A s we try to understand the process of change, we must realize that deep change comes about less because of what we try to do and how hard we try to do it, and more because of *our willingness to face the realities of our own internal life*. Personal integrity, a commitment to never pretend about anything, is prerequisite for change from the inside out.

That commitment is tough to honor. When the fullness of our disappointment drives us to an overwhelming sorrow that replaces anger with pain . . . we will be shaken to the core of our being. That kind of pain, I submit, is the starting point for real change. It is only when we face the horror of desperately longing for what no one has or ever will provide that we give up our demands of others to satisfy our thirst and we turn in humble, broken dependence to God. . . .

The painful awareness of disappointment that leads to the convicting recognition of self-protective sin is the framework within which real change can take place. The impatient desire to get "practical" advice for solving life's problems often reflects an effort to bypass the pain of an inside look. When that look is avoided, when we fail to face our deep disappointment and relational sin, then the best we can manage is superficial change. Most advice on things to do heals the wound of God's people as though it were not serious.[1]

LOOKING INSIDE

1. At this point in your study, how do you feel about the idea that taking an honest inside look is the number-one pre-

requisite for change from the inside out? Why or why not?

2. a. In what areas of your life do you still pretend that things are better than they really are?

   b. What motivates your pretense?

3. Which emotion are you most in touch with regarding the disappointment of your longings: anger or hurt?

4. a. To what extent do you feel frustrated about how to apply the lessons you've learned so far in this study?

   b. What ingredients do you feel are missing in helping you make the transition from knowledge to action?

IDENTIFYING THE PROBLEM

5. Think of a time in the past few weeks when you've been aware of problems in your world—in circumstances or relationships. Fill in the following chart, describing the various components of your response to hurt.

a. What happened?

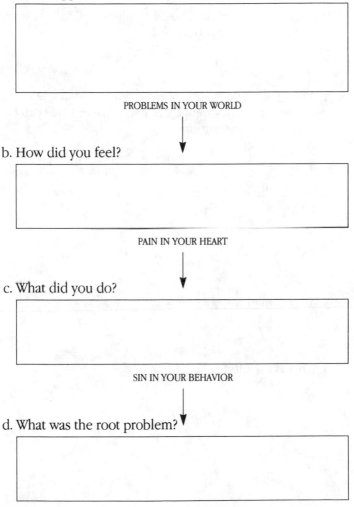

PROBLEMS IN YOUR WORLD

b. How did you feel?

PAIN IN YOUR HEART

c. What did you do?

SIN IN YOUR BEHAVIOR

d. What was the root problem?

SIN IN YOUR HEART

6. What methods of escape have you employed to avoid facing the disturbing realities of your own internal life?

7. According to Proverbs 4:23 and Matthew 15:15-20, where does the root of our problems lie?

8. a. When Jesus told the Pharisees to clean the inside of the cup and dish (Matthew 23:26), to what was He really directing their attention?

   b. What is the inside dirt in your life that must be scoured away?

9. a. What is the ultimate virtue?

   b. What is the ultimate problem?

   c. Why?

EXPLORING RELATIONSHIPS

10. Think about the person who means the most to you.

   a. In what ways has that person let you down?

   b. How do you feel about that person's failures?

   c. What is your response to that person when he or she disappoints you?

11. a. Why is facing the ways we've been victimized so crucial to recognizing the choices we make to preserve our safety with defensive patterns of relating?

   b. Describe a time in your life when your hurt as a victim caused you to be an agent of hurt—through blatant or subtle sin—in the life of another person.

12. What are three positive results of facing our disappointment in relationships?

MOVING TOWARD CHANGE

13. What do the following verses tell us about who is ultimately in control of whatever efforts we make to change from the inside out?

2 Chronicles 20:17

Psalm 57:2

Proverbs 16:9

1 Thessalonians 5:23-24

14. What relief do the following verses give to the pressure you may feel to find "Ten Easy Steps" to maturity?

Luke 8:15

Philippians 3:13-16

Hebrews 6:11-15

15. Think about a personal problem you've had—in attitude, behavior, or relationship—within the past week. Can you identify the roots of the problem? (In other words, how has being sinned against led you to sin?)

16. a. According to Matthew 16:24-25, what is the route to life?

b. Considering all that you've learned so far in this study, how would you say Jesus' words apply to your life? (What must you change in order to experience the abundant life Christ promised? Think carefully about how you define the abundant life.)

NOTE: 1. Dr. Larry Crabb, *Inside Out* (Colorado Springs, Colo.: NavPress, 1988), pages 175-176.

The Power of the Gospel

In many people's minds, change must be nearly complete, at least dramatic, or it doesn't count. And the change required to convince us we've found the secret of growth must be the change we want the most: perhaps a new set of feelings including a warm desire to love and a peaceful strength as we handle life's problems; or a deep desire to do right in the midst of temptation; or a passionate appreciation of the Lord that eliminates any feelings of despair or battles against resentment. . . .

Evangelicals sometimes expect too much or, to put it more precisely, we look for a kind of change God hasn't promised. . . . We manage to interpret biblical teaching to support our longing for perfection. As a result, we measure our progress by standards we will never meet until Heaven. . . .

. . . We therefore claim God's power as the guarantee of total change from pressure to peace, from disappointment to joy—and then live with an intolerable burden that either crushes us with despair or requires us to pretend we're better than we are. . . .

We will, of course, be flawless—one day. . . . But for now, struggles continue. There is a necessary pain of living in this world that we must simply accept. *But there are unnecessary problems that develop when we insist that necessary pain be eliminated.* Change from the inside out helps us move toward a substantial reduction in the severity and number of these unnecessary problems as we deal with the demand that energizes our self-protective maneuvering.[1]

LOOKING INSIDE

1. a. Is there some change you're waiting for as "proof" that

God is at work in your life? If so, what is it?

    b. Are you waiting for someone else to change completely before you will acknowledge the progress they have made?

2. Identify what some of the *unnecessary problems* in your life might be.

3. a. What kind of change do you believe God promises this side of Heaven?

    b. Why do you believe that?

IDENTIFYING THE PROBLEM

4. a. What is a necessary, honest response to the problems in our world?

    b. What is an unnecessary response?

5. a. Name some unnecessary problems you have created in response to the inevitable problems in your world.

   b. What is at the root of these unnecessary problems?

6. What deep motive is reflected in our determination to move away from pain through self-protective styles of relating?

7. If you believe that life is to be found in Christ and nowhere else, how is that belief reflected or compromised in your lifestyle and relationships?

EXPLORING RELATIONSHIPS

8. a. As you encourage others—friends, children, students—to grow in their Christian life, what is your primary focus?

   ___ The problems in their world
   ___ The pain in their heart
   ___ The sin in their behavior
   ___ The sin in their heart

b. What do you believe growing Christians most need to deal with in order to experience deep and lasting change?

c. Why do you think this should be the most important focus?

9. Think of a person in your life to whom it is difficult for you to be kind and loving.

a. If you make a commitment to be more loving in your next ten encounters, what do you think your success rate will be?

b. What specifically do you need to deal with, within yourself, in order to deeply change in your attitude and approach to that person?

10. a. If you maintain a stance of self-protection in your encounters with people, what are you really saying about the place comfortable, secure relationships have in your life (Matthew 10:37)?

b. How do you know when your commitment to preserve your life through self-protective styles of relating has replaced your commitment to live for Christ?

MOVING TOWARD CHANGE

11. Explain the statement, *"Without repentance, a look at Christ provides only the illusion of comfort."*

12. What does it mean to deeply repent? Very specifically, of what do you need to repent?

13. Why is it so crucial to inside-out change to have a thorough awareness of our sin, both obvious and subtle?

14. If we have truly repented, how will it affect the way we relate to people?

15. a. Write out a thorough definition of repentance.

   b. Reading back over your definition, what evidence of deep repentance do you see in your life?

NOTE: 1. Dr. Larry Crabb, *Inside Out* (Colorado Springs, Colo.: NavPress, 1988), pages 189-190.

What It Takes to Deeply Change

C hange in the Christian life is progressive. We move from *change in our conscious direction* to *change in our approach to relationships* to *change in the direction of our very being.* Each change represents a work of God and is therefore good. To label the first kind of change shallow would wrongly demean it. But to stop with the first kind of change, or the second, reflects a failure to understand the opportunity we have to pursue God and to know Him. New believers change in their conscious direction. Growing believers learn to love by abandoning their self-protection. Mature believers begin to grasp the meaning of Paul's words, "For to me, to live is Christ," as they shift the central direction of their very being toward God.[1]

LOOKING INSIDE

1. Where do you feel you are in the change process?

2. a. What do Paul's words, "For to me, to live is Christ" (Philippians 1:21), mean to you personally?

   b. How deeply do you share his understanding of where life is to be found?

3. a. How do you feel about the kind of change God is calling you to?

   b. As you near the end of this study, what is your primary emotion—excitement, anxiety, hope, discouragement, apathy, etc.? Why?

IDENTIFYING THE PROBLEM

4. What two elements must be uncovered before we can change either our conscious direction or our approach to relationships?

5. a. Give an example of a time when you shifted . . .

   your conscious direction?

   your approach to relationships?

   b. What caused the shifts in these cases?

6. What two realities must we understand if we are to have the potential for the deepest kind of change possible this side of Heaven?

7. a. What was a man designed by God to do?

   b. What was a woman designed to do?

8. What is at the core of our struggle to change from the inside out? In other words, what will a thorough inside look expose?

9. a. What is the deepest function of our self-protective maneuvering?

   b. Why is recognizing this so important to becoming all God has designed us to be?

10. Explain why fully acknowledging the unbearable sadness of life in a fallen world is so crucial to the kind of change our Lord has in mind for us.

EXPLORING RELATIONSHIPS

11. a. If you are a man, in what way do you see yourself as weakened? If you are a woman, in what way do you see yourself as damaged?

b. In what ways have you ever experienced shame in connection to your maleness or femaleness?

12. Can you recognize and describe some of the ways in which your relational style is actually functioning to preserve some sense of your sexual identity? (In other words, what do you most fear in relationships, and how do you go about protecting yourself from that?)

13. What attitudes or actions in your relationships—intimate or casual—indicate that you are not living out all you were designed to be as male or female?

MOVING TOWARD CHANGE

14. a. What emotional state precedes the deepest kind of change possible: a shift in the direction of our very being?

b. What causes this level of distress?

15. What are the results of changing the direction of our very being?

16. Think of a particularly disturbing problem in your life right now. Using all the elements of self-discovery you have learned through this study, try to trace your problem through the flowchart on the next page. (Reading the following case study may help you determine the change process in your own life.)

Are you able to discover the roots of your problem? What will it take for you to change from the inside out?

THE PROCESS OF CHANGE

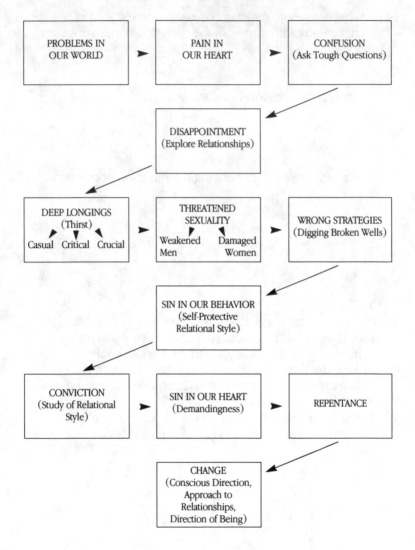

A CASE STUDY

Karen struggled with bulimia. She knew she was endangering her health and worrying her friends with her compulsion to binge and purge, but she couldn't stop.

When Karen came in for counseling, she felt hopeless over her situation. She wished she could run and hide from all the people in her life who needed her to be healthy. And she'd given up on the seemingly futile search to find the key to God's life-changing power.

During Karen's months of therapy, we looked into her background to uncover unresolved issues and explore her relationships. Among the many things we discovered were these disturbing facts: Karen's parents divorced when she was six. Being an only child, she spent the next several years emotionally, and often physically, alone as her mother withdrew into silent grief and bitterness over her broken marriage.

When Karen was twelve, her mother began dating. Within a year, Sam, her mother's boyfriend, moved into the home. Her mother withdrew even more into this new relationship. Sam seemed to be invading Karen's world, stealing not only what was left of her mother's attention, but also her privacy, her time, and her favorite chair in the living room. Eventually Sam even stole her innocence and self-respect: He sexually molested her over the next two years.

When she was fifteen, Karen's loneliness and misery drove her to drastic measures: twice she tried to take her life, and finally she ran away from home. She begged her father to take her in, but he didn't want the responsibility. She moved in with friends, and those friends led her to a personal relationship with Jesus Christ. A year later, Karen moved back in with her mother and Sam.

The next two years were painful, and Sam's sexual advances continued. Karen tried to draw comfort from her relationship with Christ. At eighteen, she left home for college. For the next four years she struggled in her Christian life, encouraged on one hand by what Christ had done for her on the cross, and baffled (*confusion*) on the other hand by His "loving" allowance of all the pain in her life (*problems in her world*). She felt overwhelming sorrow over all she had missed and given up of her childhood, and though she had many friends, she felt loved by no one (*pain in her heart*). All she wanted was to be loved for who she was and to matter in someone's life (*critical longings*), but even her own mother had let her down (*disappointment*). She felt estranged from God as well, empty at the core of her being (*crucial longings*). Though she longed for meaningful involvement with others, she was afraid to open herself up to more rejection or abuse (*threatened sexuality*).

Karen knew from her 4.0 grade point average in college that she could find a measure of fulfillment through accomplishment. She could win people's respect and involvement through performance, so she planned her career accordingly. She also had earned herself a reputation as a good listener. Her friends relied on her support and advice. That, too, brought a measure of fullness to her soul. At least she had two skills she could depend upon (*wrong strategies*) to bring her some level of comfort.

Over the next few years, Karen won herself a lot of strokes through her competence and caring (*relational style*). It never occurred to her that her style was designed to keep her from experiencing further pain in her relationships (*self-protection*), much less that her attractive interaction with others involved sinful motivation (*sin in her behavior*).

By the time she was thirty, Karen had nearly reached the pinnacle of success in her profession. She had countless friends depending on her for help and support. Yet she'd never felt so empty.

Turning thirty had been hard. Even though her painful relationships with Sam and her dad had soured her on the idea of marriage (*damaged femaleness*), she longed for companionship. She'd learned that God was there for her; He'd blessed her in many ways. But He never seemed to be enough to fill the bottomless void in her soul.

Food was a momentary comfort on many a lonely evening. In fact, food had been a comfort during childhood, too. But Karen's nightly snacks were getting to be irresistible. The snacks became second dinners, whole bags of potato chips, pints of ice cream. One night, disgusted with herself after another binge, she put her finger down her throat and threw up. Not only did she feel better physically, but she felt tremendous emotional relief. She could control the consequences of her out-of-control behavior. Finally, she could control *something* in her life.

But the binging and purging got the best of Karen. Her health began to suffer. Some of her friends figured out what was going on. She felt ashamed, hopeless, and victimized. Her compulsion now controlled *her.*

Karen's healing and change came slowly. But once she thoroughly reviewed her thirty-one years of life—the problems, pain, confusion, disappointment, unmet longings, damaged sexuality, wrong strategies, and self-protection—she could begin to see what lay underneath. She moved from bitterness and fear to *conviction* over the unloving ways she'd related to people and the *demandingness* that fueled her approach to life. She saw that her demand that life be more comfortable, God be more fair, and people be more perfect had trapped her behind defensive walls of competence and strength—walls that kept her from experiencing the joy of drinking deeply from her relationship with God and truly giving herself to the people she cared about.

Karen's grief over the root of her sin motivated a change of direction (*repentance*). Not only did her eating habits slowly come back into balance (*change in her conscious direction*), but her walls began to come down with her friends, and even with her family (*change in her approach to relationships*). She still felt frequently disappointed in people's responses to her, but her conviction that genuinely loving others was vital to life kept her tearing down the walls almost as fast as she'd put them up.

The greatest change in Karen showed up in her relationship with the Lord. The more directly she faced the pain in her life, the more she ached, and the more she ached, the more she began to see God as her one and only hope (*change in the direction of her very being*).

Karen today is a woman of passion and vitality. She still questions and hurts and fails, but with each year she gains a greater measure of faith and hope and love. Karen is changing from the inside out.

NOTE: 1. Dr. Larry Crabb, *Inside Out* (Colorado Springs, Colo.: NavPress, 1988), pages 202-203.